POSITIVELY DIFFERENT

POSITIVELY DIFFERENT

CREATING A BIAS-FREE ENVIRONMENT
FOR YOUNG CHILDREN

Ana Consuelo Matiella, MA

Suggestions for teachers, parents and other care providers
of children to age 10

Network Publications, a division of ETR Associates
Santa Cruz, CA
1991

10 9 8 7 6 5 4 3 2

Printed in the United States of America

Illustrations by Marcia Quackenbush
Design by Julia Chiapella

Library of Congress Cataloging-in-Publication Data

Matiella, Ana Consuelo.
    Positively different : creating a bias-free environment for
young children / Ana Consuelo Matiella.
        p.   cm.
    "Suggestions for teachers, parents, and other care providers
of children to age 10."
    Includes bibliographical references.
    ISBN 1-56071-059-4
    1. Prejudices in children—United States. 2. Prejudices—
Study and teaching (Elementary) United States. 3. Self-percep-
tion in children. I. Title.
BF723.P75M37   1991
305'.083—dc20   91-20022
                                                          CIP

Title No. 509

I would like to dedicate this book to my mother and father for turning out a multicultural product and to the people in Nogales, Arizona, who taught me about borders and how to cross them.

"Unless...educators learn to prize and value differences and to view them as resources for learning, neither whites nor minority groups will experience the teaching and learning situations best suited to prepare them to live effectively in a world whose population is characterized by diversity."

—Gerald J. Pine and Asa G. Hilliard III
"Rx for Racism: Imperatives
for America's Schools"
Phi Delta Kappan (April 1990)

Contents

Preface

I recently had the opportunity to help at the elementary school where my daughter, Sara, goes to school. The day was full of excitement. The second grade teachers had organized a thematic teaching day around apples. I never knew you could do so many things with apples!

The day was structured so that all the second graders in the school came through our classroom. I was assigned to help with the tissue and construction paper mobile activity—an apple, of course.

In one of my groups, I noticed a little girl staring at me and looking down at her paper. She looked up, then down several times before I caught her eye and smiled at her. She finally decided to ask me her question, "Are you Chinese or Korean?"

"I am Spanish and Mexican, how about you," I replied. She said, "I'm Japanese and Korean."

Her name was Amy. She then told me that her mother was Korean and didn't speak English. Her father was Japanese and he spoke English. I told her my mother didn't speak English either. We shared our respective immigrant stories and she finished her red and green apple mobile.

What impressed me about this conversation was that Amy knew, by observing me for just a few minutes, that I was different from the rest of the adults who were there that day.

I thought about my conversation with Amy for the next few days. Perhaps she could tell I was "different" because she was "different." Perhaps not. We did establish a common bond, though. Both of us *were* different. We connected on our ethnicity.

Children know about differences and they know how differences are perceived and evaluated by the people in their environment. Very early in their development they know there are values assigned to differences.

They know, for example, that light skin is more valued than dark skin. They know that being fat means other kids won't like you as much. They know there is preferred status in driving a BMW rather than a Toyota. They know that being male is considered more powerful than being female. They know about the hammers and the nails. I'm sorry they know, but they know.

Seeking to change messages about differences from negative to positive is an enormous challenge. Adults who care for young children have tremendous power to shape the way they perceive and respond to the world around them. I welcome this opportunity to support parents, teachers and other caring adults in creating a safe place where children can begin to build a world where difference is honored.

I would like to express my gratitude to all the educators and change agents who are committed to moving us to a higher plane, to a place where all children are acknowledged and celebrated. The issues dealt with in this book are not new. There is a great body of knowledge and work that has already been done in this field. My task in writing this book was to draw from this body of knowledge and apply the concepts to enhancing the learning environment, at school and at home. I am humbly grateful to those who came before me, and acknowledge their help and guidance.

I would also like to thank Kay Clark, editor extraordinaire, for making editing seem easy, when I know it's not.

Changing Messages About Difference

By the year 2000 over a third of the students in our nation's schools will be labeled ethnic minority students. To date, this label means they are African American, Hispanic/Latino, Native American or Asian/Pacific Islander. Although cultural diversity in the schools is a national trend, some states like California, New Mexico, and Texas are already at the 50% or higher mark.

We admit that our educational system is failing a large number of our students, especially our ethnic students. We continue to "blame the victims" by saying that home life, economic status, lack of English language skills, or cultural deprivation are preventing them from achieving.

The fact is that for many children of color, the education that they are receiving is irrelevant. We are only now beginning to explore the possibility that our monocultural approach is not reaching our multicultural audience.

The *El No* Model

Roberto Vargas and Samuel Martinez, in their classic *Razalogia: Community Learning for a New Society* (Razagente Associates, 1984), provide a model that is appropriate to reflect on in this introduction. "El No and the Raza Child" appropriately applies to all ethnic children who feel disempowered and alienated in our schools and in our society.

There are three influencing factors in the *El No* model: professional encounters, media and school. The child is in the middle as the receiver of the messages from the influencing factors. *"El No"* illustrates the sense of disempowerment and lack of self worth that a child feels who finds no reflection of him- or herself outside the home.

In encounters with professionals, be they teachers, counselors, librarians, doctors, healthworkers, or mailcarriers, if there are no role models, if there is no one the child is like, the message is *"No puedes"*— "You can't."

In the media (i.e., television, movies, magazines, books), if there are no role models, if there is no one the child can see him- or herself in, the message is *"No vales"*— "You have no worth."

PROFESSIONAL ENCOUNTERS

No puedes - you can't.

MEDIA

No vales - you have no worth.

• NO RAZA ROLE MODELS

• NO RAZA ROLE MODELS

No puedo - I can't.

No valgo - I have no worth.

SCHOOL

No puedes - you can't.

• LACK OF RAZA ROLE MODELS
• LACK OF CULTURE/LANGUAGE SENSITIVITY
• LACK OF VALIDATING CURRICULUM

Adapted with permission from Robert Vargas.

In the schools, where there is a dearth of teachers and other role models from ethnic backgrounds, where often there is a lack of culture and language sensitivity, and where there is no validating curriculum, the child receives the same message: *"No puedes"*— "You can't."

These messages aren't always direct or blatant. They are the subtle and powerful messages of exclusion and rejection that the child absorbs. The child's sad conclusion is one of low self-worth and disempowerment. *"No puedo"*— "I can't." *"No valgo"*— "I have no worth."

Although the *El No* model addresses ethnicity, attitudes toward differences aren't limited to ethnic groups. Discrimination based on differences also arises because of gender, sexual orientation, weight, and physical and mental abilities. The messages are the same.

A first step in changing these negative messages is to change the way we perceive differences. The logical place to start is with the children. The early childhood and primary education setting is an ideal place to teach children about the diversity of the world we live in. These early years, when children are developing their social skills, is the best time to plant the seeds of acceptance and respect for others. Here we can teach about differences from a positive point of view. Differences can be presented as qualities that make us unique and special.

Teaching Children About Differences

For decades, and slowly, we have been moving beyond merely acknowledging that we are a multicultural nation toward striving to be a pluralistic one. A multicultural nation is one in which people from many cultures share a common living place, but not everyone takes part equally. In a pluralistic nation, all people have the opportunity to contribute and participate without sacrificing their language, ethnicity or culture.

In a pluralistic society, all children can find their reflections in the mirrors of the media, the schools and the workplace. They see positive role models on TV, in movies and in ads. There are teachers, principals, doctors and community leaders they identify with. They can find validation and inspiration all around them. They can find the *"Sí puedes"* and the *"Sí vales"*—the "Yes, you can," the "Yes, you are worthy."

To accomplish this ideal, we need to examine our attitudes about differences honestly and closely. And we need to help children understand four basic things about differences:

❦ Differences exist.

❦ Differences are good.

❦ Unjust treatment of differences exists.

❦ Unjust treatment of differences is wrong.

Teaching children that differences exist and that unjust treatment of differences exists is a first essential step toward change. This acknowledges and validates what many children already know: as Kermit the Frog so succinctly puts it, "It's not easy being green." For children who haven't experienced discrimination or prejudice, understanding these concepts can plant the seeds for valuable prevention education.

By teaching young children that differences are good, we help them celebrate differences from the beginning. We invite them to discover uniqueness and all the gifts that come with that discovery.

And finally, by taking a firm stand against the unjust treatment of differences, we model behavior that will affect their lives.

Where Do We Begin?

To begin to give children positive messages about differences, we need to keep some basic questions in mind:

- ❦ How do we help children recognize differences as positive and deal with them in appropriate ways?

- ❦ How do we acknowledge unjust treatment without perpetuating the victim role?

- ❦ How do we move positively from a place of hurt to a place of healing?

- ❦ How do we challenge myths that limit children's potential and keep them trapped by stereotypes and low expectations?

- ❦ How do we move beyond prejudice with conviction and commitment?

I hope you can begin to accomplish the following goals as you work with children:

- ❦ Give *"Sí se puede"*— "Yes, you can"—messages to children. Begin to reverse *"El No."*

- ❦ Help children accept, respect and celebrate differences.

- ❦ Give all children the means to protect themselves from discrimination.

I believe one key to achieving these ideal goals is to create a learning environment as close as possible to the world as we wish it could be—a place where children can feel safe and can learn by example and by practice what it means to live in a world where differences are explored, accepted and respected.

The focus of this book is how we as teachers, parents and guides can counter *"El No"* in the environments that we influence. Its intent is to provide information and ideas for creating a bias-free environment where children can learn to deal with differences in a positive manner.

What Is a Bias-Free Environment?

A bias-free learning environment is one in which the diversity of the world we live in is reflected in a way that doesn't exclude or stereotype anyone on the basis of skin color, ethnicity, gender, age, class or physical ability.

It is an environment where diversity is reflected in the physical setting: where the walls, posters, books, materials, dolls, games, songs and other teaching tools are carefully selected to acknowledge, accept and welcome the idea that each of us is different and that differences are good.

It is a safe environment, where there is an atmosphere of caring and respect for every child's way of being in the world. There are clear rules that protect the rights of children to ask questions, have opinions, and be accepted and respected for who they are.

It is an environment where each child is esteemed—and therefore gains esteem—based on how he or she is unique and different individually and culturally.

It is an environment that supports those children who might be recognizing for the first time that values of friends and classmates are different from those they've learned at home. It is a place where they can find guidance to develop skills to sort through the sometimes complex issues of ethnic/cultural awareness and pride.

Some children may be having their first experiences with meeting or socializing with friends from different backgrounds. A bias-free learning environment introduces them to differences through positive experiences that can shape their attitudes for the rest of their lives.

Who Needs to Learn About Differences?

Learning how to deal with differences is a crucial skill all children need to survive and thrive in our society. If not dealt with positively, differences can result in children with low self-esteem, who are alienated from one another and in conflict. And all children are negatively affected by disrespect for differences, whether they are the targets or the perpetrators of prejudice and the discrimination that results from it.

Those who have already been hurt by prejudice and discrimination need to have their experiences named and validated, so they can move beyond the hurt to a place of healing and growth.

Those children who have not experienced prejudice and discrimination need to be introduced to the concepts and the consequences, and to understand that unjust treatment of differences is not acceptable behavior.

At the purest level is our deep desire that children learn to live together in harmony and respect, that they grow up as bias-free as possible. For this to happen, we need to teach all children the critical thinking skills they need to function with depth and awareness in a diverse world. Ignoring differences does not teach these skills. Rather, it keeps us in a state of ignorance, fear and denial.

Let's look more closely at the "we are all the same" idea. If being the same is the ideal, then being different is less than being the same. If the media presents blond-haired, blue-eyed women as the ideal, the unspoken message is that brunettes are less than blondes. When men are represented as the ones "in charge," the unspoken message is that women are less powerful. When most major television personalities are Anglo, the message is that being Anglo is preferable to being a person of color.

There are messages within mainstream culture that we need to examine and help our children examine. Hidden messages once considered harmless are charged with judgments about what is good and what is not, what makes the grade and what does not. We need to help children be aware and critical of hidden messages and examine these messages in a way that will help them to be more empathetic and caring people. We need to commit ourselves to challenging the silent and not so silent no's that children who are different encounter.

Who Can Use This Book?

As adults who care for young children, we have tremendous power to shape the way they perceive and respond to the world around them. This is a book for adults who influence children.

There are many different approaches and motivating factors to consider when teaching children about differences. Perhaps you are a teacher with a class that is predominantly children of color and you notice there is some ambivalence about how children feel about their skin color and other physical traits. Perhaps you have heard some "slurs" on the playground. Perhaps in your predominantly White classroom, you notice a discomfort about differences.

If you are a parent, perhaps your child has already come to you with questions or stories about discriminatory behavior in the neighborhood or classroom. You may have overheard a child making a hurtful remark to another child. Perhaps you are concerned about the reported increases of racially motivated violence among young people. How do we respond to children's behavior that reflects larger issues in the society in which we live?

All children need positive messages about differences, and all children need to see those positive messages reflected in the environments in which they live and learn. The more teachers, parents and others strive to see that as many positive concepts as possible are in place in the home, the school, and in every program where young children learn, the closer we will come to realizing a bias-free ideal in the larger environment we live in.

Although a focus of this book is on helping teachers create a safe and bias-free environment for children, the suggestions, information and messages can also be used in the home by parents and other caregivers. Parents acting as partners with their children's teachers will find the book useful as well.

What You Will Find in This Book

The intent of this book is to offer background information and practical suggestions for creating a bias-free learning environment in the classroom or home where all children can feel safe and proud to be who they are, and where they are taught to respect differences in others.

For our purposes, the focus of this book is on ethnic differences. But openness, respect and acceptance for ethnic differences easily translates into the same positive attitudes toward differences in physical appearance and/or abilities, class, age, sexual orientation, gender and so on.

Chapter 1 discusses why it is important to help children recognize, understand and accept differences in themselves and in others. The importance of acknowledging differences, as opposed to the "color blind approach," and the need to redefine "different" to mean something positive are explored. Background information and the history of attitudes about differences in our society are briefly examined, and some model elementary school programs that teach the value of difference are discussed.

Chapter 2 includes suggestions for preparing to implement a bias-free environment. Here are guidelines for looking closely at possible personal biases that could interfere with effective bias-free teaching. Here, too, are suggestions for the footwork, the preplanning preparations that will make the actual anti-bias environment easier to create and implement. Getting to know the children you work with and their families, understanding your community, and anticipating cultural issues that might arise when talking about specific subjects are discussed in this chapter. This chapter is useful for assessing the "ethnic awareness level" in both the school and the home.

In Chapter 3, careful attention is given to creating a physical environment where children can feel safe and at home. The chapter discusses things to think about when building this environment: what to put on walls where children learn and play, and how to choose toys, books, music, literature and games to create a physical environment that reflects diversity.

Chapter 4 discusses the more abstract but no less important elements of establishing a bias-free learning environment: how to ensure an atmosphere of caring and respect, increase children's self-esteem through pride in themselves and their ethnicity and culture, and help them develop and practice critical thinking skills.

Chapter 5 discusses what to do when prevention efforts don't prevent prejudice and discrimination. Despite all the best efforts, hurtful incidents will still happen. When they do, they can be used to assess what kind of action needs to be taken, what direction the anti-bias teaching needs to take. These "red-flag" incidents can open doors to discussions about differences that can have a positive influence on the lives of the children involved.

These are enormous issues. In effecting social change it is easy to get overwhelmed by the scope of the problems. But remember that we don't need to have all the answers before we can effectively educate children about these sensitive issues. The solutions lie in raising the questions, and in being willing to confront the issues.

Also, it is important to remind ourselves that every small victory matters. No single book, teacher, parent, or school will magically change the way we relate to one another. But every book, every teacher, every parent and every school can *begin* to make a difference.

Chapter 1

The Trouble with Denying Differences

One night while writing this book, I turned on the television and tuned into a news show. Several young men and women were being interviewed in New York City, where there had been ugly incidents of racial violence. As I watched, I felt pride, compassion and sympathy for these young people. It was obvious that they were concerned; the worry was visible on their faces. They were looking for solutions.

A young African American woman said something that was appropriate for me to hear as I was writing a book on differences. She said, "I can't understand prejudice because, really, we are all the same."

We Aren't All the Same

It occurred to me that here was one of our problems. In our society, being different has been defined as something negative. We have actively promoted the "we are all the same" ideal—also referred to as the "color blind approach." Without bad intentions, in an attempt to deal with differences in a positive manner, we have denied differences and promoted the value of "sameness."

But we *aren't* all the same. And ignoring our differences is not yielding the positive results we once expected. Ignoring differences has resulted in feelings of exclusion and inadequacy in children of color and a warped sense of what is real, not only in children of color, but in all children.

Denying differences is denying a part of yourself. When we deny that children are different we could be denying them the right to fully emerge as whole human beings.

A personal example illustrates this point. I am a Spanish-Mexican Latina. In the environment in which I was raised a higher value was assigned to being a Spaniard than to being Mexican. In turn, being Mexican was of higher value than being Indian.

My father (the Spaniard) knew the score and always encouraged Spanish cultural pride. My mother somewhat reluctantly encouraged us to own our Mexican heritage. She did so while underplaying the fact that, by definition, if we were Mexicans, then we were Indians too.

As I grew into adulthood I found I couldn't deny my ethnic identity in all its complexity. To deny my Indian blood was to deny an integral part of who I am in my soul of souls.

My experience wasn't unique. For many of us the melting pot is not a workable alternative. A classic reclaiming of ethnic pride is the African American assertion that "Black is beautiful." Although the phrase seems dated now, the idea is as important today as it was during the civil rights movement of the sixties.

Each child brings to any situation his or her own reality, values and culture. All teaching and learning takes place in a sociocultural context. Every day in our classrooms we actively socialize students and pass on values. Historically we have done this from a foundation based on Western European culture. Consciously or unconsciously we have taught, and sometimes continue to teach, that western civilization and culture are superior and therefore dominant.

Subsequently, when we look for ways we are alike, we look for traits, values and images that match mainstream traits, values and images. To ask a child of color to look for how we are alike is potentially alienating because "alike" is measured in terms that do not necessarily apply to him or her.

Looking for similarities and ignoring differences turns out to be a ploy, whether we acknowledge it or not, to transform all children into reflections of a mainstream image. Since the ethnic child will never exactly fit this image, this undermines his or her identity. The child's own unique identity, his or her own reflection in the mirror is not validated or reinforced. This is the *El No* model discussed in the introduction.

In the *El No* model, the mainstream values are reflected and therefore validated. Values that are different are not reflected; they are ignored at best and attacked at worst. It is disabling and destructive for children of color to constantly be required to make their reflection fit someone else's image. Our challenge as parents and teachers is to help all children find their own unique reflection in the mirror—and value it. To do this, two things have to happen.

First, we need to help children form a strong sense of self-esteem that incorporates an equally strong ethnic or group identity. This is particularly important with children of color because many of them are already dealing with group- and self-identities that have been battered by racism.

Second, we need to help children understand that differences are a reality in our society. Because of the way we have socialized our children at home, in the media and in the classroom, an Anglo child in an English-speaking monocultural classroom may be at higher risk of being "culturally illiterate" than a child in a multicultural classroom. Thus we need to reach out in special ways to help these children understand and define differences positively, and accept and respect each other.

Anti-Bias Education at School

The school is a logical place for children to learn these concepts, the earlier the better. School may be the first place where a child experiences the idea of difference in its many facets, so the opportunity for experiential teaching is present. The environment is one where learning takes place, so lessons about differences can easily be integrated into the core curriculum. And school is the place where some of the most important adults in the child's life—parents and teachers—can work together to shape future values and perspectives.

Two multicultural and anti-bias publications come to mind that strive to place validation and positive reflections in the schools.

In their book, *Ethnic Pride* (Good Apple, Inc., 1983), Greta Barclay Lipson and Jane A. Romatowski present ideas and information that help students explore a wide range of cultures, especially their own. Children can choose their group from a list of 97 different ethnic groups in the United States, or they can add their own group if it doesn't appear on the list.

The book's 16 chapters explore topics like names, rituals, foods, medicine and superstition, language, famous people, fashion, geography and history. Each chapter has information for the teacher, student activity suggestions and a research project that asks students to interview parents, grandparents, etc., to gather information about the topic as it pertains to their own culture. Although the book is for grades 4-9, the material is easy to adapt. Many of the ideas can work for younger children.

An activity in the rituals chapter asks students to find out how the birth of children is announced in their culture. For example, in the United States, the parents may pass out cigars, lollipops, pens, etc., while Belgians may use sugar-coated almonds. In the chapter on names, children learn to write their names in the language of their ancestors, and to pronounce their ancestral name out loud. Candies from different cultures are studied in the chapter on foods.

The authors of *Ethnic Pride* have chosen topics that are easy to personalize, thus making some fairly abstract ideas concrete and understandable for young children.

Another excellent resource for teaching children about differences is an activity-oriented handbook for educators of children in grades K-5 developed by the Madison, Wisconsin, public school system. *Individual Differences: An Experience in Human Relations for Children* was developed by Madison's Individual Differences Program in 1974 and is distributed through the Anti-Defamation League of B'nai B'rith in New York City.

The handbook is designed around eight objectives in five sections. In sections about the human family, individual differences, emotions and feelings, and prejudice and cultural differences, educators are guided through a program of 270 activities that help teach young children respect for differences. The program is guided by nine sequential objectives and founded on a "layered" learning approach. This means the first eight objectives, in sequence, are intended to lay the groundwork for teaching the final objective, prejudice and cultural differences.

The key to the Wisconsin material is that differences are used as a way to unite with others. Indeed, the one area that can be considered a commonality is the fact that we are all different. We all contribute uniquely to the richness of the world. So although finding things in common with others is one way to bond, the program stresses that bridging activities based on commonalities will work more effectively after children have positively defined differences and learned to accept and respect diversity among human beings.

In summary, there are three reasons why we as teachers can't ignore differences and must take care not to pressure children to match prescribed mainstream identities.

- ❧ Ignoring differences denies the emergence of self.

- ❧ Ignoring differences hinders self-esteem and self-identity.

- ❧ Ignoring differences does a grave disservice to children. Children taught to ignore differences lack the skills they need to live in today's multifaceted and diverse world.

I think back to that young African American woman on television, struggling to make sense of the meaning of racist violence, and I change her response. This time she says, "I don't understand prejudice because although we are all different, we all deserve the same respect and dignity. We deserve to see our own multicolored images in the mirror." The goal of the following chapters is to help make it possible for all children to understand differences as positively as my re-educated young woman.

Chapter 2

Behind the Scenes:
Exploring Hidden Agendas

To give children positive messages about differences, we need to make sure our own behavior reflects what we hope to teach. This chapter will help you explore your own attitudes about differences and think in advance about issues that might come up as you work to develop your bias-free learning environment.

Many of the following concepts and ideas were adapted from *Family Life Education in Multicultural Classrooms: Practical Guidelines* (ETR Associates/Network Publications, 1990). The guidelines were developed in response to requests from teachers who wanted to make family life education culturally and ethnically relevant and appropriate for a diverse classroom. Most of the general concepts work well for teachers of young children.

I think of the issues in this chapter as the "hidden agenda" of anti-bias education. If we have been trained in the color blind approach to differences—and many of us have—we haven't acknowledged many of the following issues, let alone studied them. Don't worry if some of these areas seem beyond the scope of your work with children. Just being aware that they exist will help you begin to open doors to a positive approach to differences that will have a profound effect.

Know Your Biases

All of us were raised with certain prejudices and we must face them in order to get past them. If we don't face them we won't get through the blocks. We are more likely to act out prejudices if we remain in denial. Acknowledging that we all have prejudices allows us to move on from there.

Uncomfortable feelings arise when we deal with people and things that are different from us. These feelings often come from fear of the unknown and from our sincere belief that our way is the best way. One important thing we can do as parents and teachers is be willing to become aware of these feelings in ourselves. Once we reach this level of awareness of ourselves, it is easier to recognize uncomfortable feelings in children, and to help them see that the feelings are often a clue from inside that we need to learn more about the world around us.

Answering the following questions may help you identify ways you unintentionally show biases*:

1. Which five students do I most like and feel most comfortable with? Which five do I least like and feel least comfortable with?

2. Do these students have anything in common with each other, e.g., dress, language, behavior, cleanliness, manners, culture, ethnicity?

3. Can I identify a bias that is indicated by their similarities?

4. Have I arranged the room so the better or brighter students are closer to me and/or have the best view of the chalkboard?

5. When I need a teacher's helper, do I tend to ask the same few students every time? Do I give smarter students or students from certain cultural/ethnic groups more class privileges?

6. Do I spend more instructional time with one group of students than others?

7. Do I give high achievers more time to respond to questions? Am I more impatient and quicker to give answers to low achievers?

*Adapted with permission from *The Prejudice Book: Activities for the Classroom.* 1979. David A. Sherman. New York: Anti-Defamation League of B'nai B'rith.

8. Do I tend to expect less from certain students? If so, do these students have anything in common? Are they economically disadvantaged, and/or members of an ethnic group? Do they achieve less?

9. Do I praise or encourage (verbal and written comments) certain students more than others? Are the well-praised students from any particular economic, ethnic or cultural group?

Remember that ignoring differences doesn't make them go away. It increases resistance to developing acceptance and respect for others. Once aware of your feelings, you can move on to create experiences that build comfort, acceptance and respect for diversity.

Know Your Students

Getting to know the children in your classroom as individuals and as members of different groups is one of the most important things you can do to begin to facilitate an exchange of ideas and acceptance of the unique gift that each child brings to your classroom. Draw from your students' experience. Do any of your students speak languages other than English? Would they be willing to teach the class to sing a song in their "other language"? Do you have students who have lived in another country, or who have families who do? Can they bring photographs of their "other country family" and talk about what these family members eat for breakfast or what they study in school?

Give a clear message to the families of the children you work with that you need their help in enriching the classroom and school environment. (See Chapter 4 for specific suggestions for involving parents.)

As much as possible your learning environment should reflect the diversity in your community. If you live in a segregated area, connect with those parts of your community that aren't represented in your classroom. This will not only add depth to your teaching style and approach, it will model to your students the importance of reaching out to others in a positive way.

Never lose sight of the fact that you are creating an environment that promotes acceptance and respect for diversity. If there are no children of color in your classroom or community, it is even more important to strive to reflect the diversity we have in the United States.

A range of values, beliefs and attitudes exists within ethnic groups. Always assume that this range may reflect views held by your students' families. This means making sure classroom discussions reflect diversity, and modeling for students the willingness to hear ideas different than your own. Remember to

🍎 Be sensitive to the possibility that biases may exist among students and that parents may hold the same biases.

🍎 Be aware in helping children understand and overcome stereotypes that this process is quicker for some than for others.

🍎 Respect and reinforce the cultural perspectives of your students. Refer them to their parents or other significant adults for additional information and guidance.

Topics to Think About

It isn't realistic to expect yourself never to make a mistake about ethnic issues when interacting with young children. Thinking in advance about issues that might come up around a particular topic can help you avoid surprises. Following is a partial list of sample topics that might be expected to come up in situations that involve young children. Although specific to the topics, the suggestions offer a model that could also be more generally applied to a number of subjects.

Families

When preparing lessons and talking to young children about families, remember to

- ❦ Stress that there are many definitions of what a family is. Definitions depend on individual experiences and ethnic backgrounds.

- ❦ Present and validate families in a variety of forms. Be sure to include the different family forms of all the children you work with.

- ❦ Keep in mind that parenting styles, forms of discipline and expressions of affection vary within various families according to their ethnicity and culture.

- ❦ Emphasize the importance of the family as a source of support and encouragement.

- ❦ Be aware of different roles and expectations children might feel as a part of growing up male or female in their families, their ethnic culture and the larger culture in which they interact. Cultural background can affect one's perception and experience of being male or female.

- ❦ Be aware that children's families may be experiencing intergenerational stress and value conflicts among members if grandparents, parents and children are integrating into main-stream society at different levels.

- ❦ Encourage communication between students and their parents to help overcome barriers.

- ❦ Support the active involvement of parents as the primary values educators of their children.

Self-Esteem

When dealing with issues of self-esteem, remember to

- ❦ Recognize the importance of self-esteem as a factor in the achievement of academic and personal goals. (See Chapter 4 for a discussion of self-esteem as it applies to educating children about differences.)

- ❦ Promote a sense of connection among children by developing a climate of mutual respect.

- ❦ Encourage students to see themselves as unique and worth-while individuals within the context of their ethnic heritage.

- ❦ Empower children by teaching personal responsibility and control over the direction of their lives.

- ❦ Be aware that many families consider the needs of the group over the needs of the individual. Reinforce the concept of power centered in the family as well as in the individual.

- ❦ Introduce visible role models of leadership and success from different ethnic backgrounds. Encourage students to set and pursue goals and to become leaders.

Cultural Pride

In helping children gain and keep a sense of pride in their own ethnicity and culture, remember to

- 🍎 Be aware that cultural pride is essential to the self-esteem and achievement of children.

- 🍎 Recognize that children live within the context of their cultural framework and at the same time are uniquely apart from it.

- 🍎 Help children understand that some values are commonly held by all cultures, and that there are values, traditions and beliefs unique to specific cultures.

- 🍎 Help children begin to understand that while people from a distinct cultural and ethnic group may generally hold certain values in common, particular families and individuals may not share the common values.

- 🍎 Create a climate of acceptance and affirmation of differences.

Skills for Change

When teaching children to respect and value differences in themselves and in others, certain skills for change can be useful. Help children begin to

- 🍎 Integrate the personal and cultural aspects of themselves. This begins to happen when children are taught to be proud of their ethnicity and are encouraged to share aspects of their culture with the rest of the class.

🐾 Recognize and understand the concept of stereotyping and begin to learn skills to respond to and prevent it. (See Chapter 5.)

🐾 Learn to communicate effectively with friends, teachers, family and others.

When helping children communicate, remember that not all cultures share the belief that the best way to communicate is by open discussion of feelings. Avoid setting rigid standards or models of communication that do not respect cultural norms and styles. (See Chapter 4 for a discussion about different ways to express feelings.)

Making Decisions

Students who learn the elements of decision making from a very young age have an advantage when it comes to achieving life goals. When helping young children develop decision-making skills, remember that

🐾 Different options in decision making depend on one's cultural background and perspectives (e.g., resources, power, skills).

🐾 The best decision for the same situation may be different for each student based on experience and cultural background.

🐾 The consequences of an action or decision may be seen differently by children based on their experience and their cultural background.

🐾 Exploring the consequences of a decision with children should include discussing how the decision might affect their families and their relationship with family members.

❦ The ability to implement decisions is influenced by one's ethnic background as well as status in society, economic or educational levels, language, and resources.

❦ Students should be encouraged to consider family values as well as individual strengths and desires when making decisions.

This has been a chapter full of questions and general information to help you begin to recognize some of the ways anti-bias teaching might differ from your regular learning environment. Perhaps you are already aware of all the issues raised here. I applaud you! Perhaps you discovered some new ideas you can share with children. In either case, now that you have done your homework, you are ready to set your bias-free stage!

Chapter 3

Walls, Dolls and Stories: Creating a Bias-Free Classroom

We have discussed the feelings of exclusion and invalidation that result when children can't see themselves in the mirrors of the world they live in. As adults, we create many mirrors in which children see themselves. Television sets are mirrors. Magazines are mirrors. Books, dolls and puppets are mirrors. And classrooms are mirrors.

I think of the elementary classroom as an incubator in which children can grow and develop at their own pace, in their own way. As teachers we have a rare opportunity to provide a nurturing and accepting place for them to learn.

In a bias-free learning environment, we can help children develop a solid foundation on which to build healthy perceptions. We can bring them along from the beginning rather than challenging misconceptions once they've been formed. If we teach them well now, we won't have to go back and try to fix problems that may arise from intolerance later on.

The environment includes the curriculum. It includes the physical environment—the classroom, school library, multipurpose room, cafeteria, administrative offices and all other common areas of the school. It includes the tools and strategies you use to help you in your teaching.

The Curriculum

In the primary grades, the core curriculum areas of emphasis such as language arts and social studies are ideal for teaching about differences and respect for diversity. Multicultural ideas and concepts can be explored. At the same time critical thinking skills can be applied to challenge misconceptions, question stereotypes and understand prejudice. All these concepts and ideas can be easily integrated into the core curriculum.

To evaluate whether your curriculum responds to and reflects the ethnic and cultural diversity of your students and of society, ask yourself the following questions*:

1. Do the books and other materials I intend to use include different groups (e.g., ethnicity, sex, age, different physical and learning abilities, class)? Do they treat different groups honestly, realistically and sensitively?

2. Have I learned who the children I work with are? How do I plan to use their backgrounds, values and ways of thinking to improve my instruction?

3. When developing my goals and strategies, have I considered the different cultures and learning styles of the children I work with?

4. Does my curriculum help the children I work with learn to function effectively in different cultures?

5. Does my curriculum help strengthen children's sense of identity? Does it help them understand themselves better in light of their own heritage?

6. Does my curriculum include discussions about prejudice and discrimination?

7. Does my curriculum include both positive and negative aspects of ethnic group experiences?

*Adapted with permission from *Curriculum Guidelines for Multiethnic Education: Position Statement.* 1976. Arlington, VA: National Council for the Social Studies.

8. Does my curriculum help children understand that there are similarities and differences within as well as among different groups?

9. How do I plan to help children separate facts from opinions?

10. Have I planned how I will spot and then help dispel misconceptions, stereotypes and prejudices that children appear to hold?

11. Do I introduce children to persons of varying backgrounds and occupations within different groups?

12. Do I help students understand that different groups might perceive the same events or situations very differently?

13. Do I encourage children to take action on social problems they are concerned about?

The Holiday Approach: Pros and Cons

It is worth mentioning here that integration is an important goal in multicultural education. Multicultural concepts are often introduced only at "special" times, such as Cinco de Mayo, Chinese New Year, African Heritage Week, and other "Holidays Around the World." This is sometimes called "the Holiday Approach" to teaching multiculturalism.

The value of the holiday approach is somewhat obvious—it's fun, it usually centers around holidays, and children can learn about each other's cultures and customs in the true spirit of celebration. The limitation of the holiday approach is that it can trivialize cultures and customs in a way that isolates groups, setting them aside as novel or quaint.

If the holiday approach is the only multicultural education children receive, it can contribute to tokenism by, for example, dealing with prejudice and discrimination only once a year during Martin Luther King's birthday, or looking at Chinese American contributions only during the Chinese New Year festivities. In other words, if we only promote bias-free thinking in our children during holidays, we are not really educating them about the depth of our diverse world and the importance of a pluralistic contribution to our nation. We need to go beyond the holiday approach, into the whats, whos, hows and whys of diversity.

Having said that, I also feel there is a place for such frivolity and fun. The holiday approach is a great opportunity to teach children multicultural concepts such as different traditions and celebrations, how we are different and how we are similar.

One way to incorporate the holiday approach into your environment is to concentrate on the universal themes that are characteristic of so many holidays around the world. For example, the winter solstice is a winter holiday theme centering around darkness and light. Darkness and light have importance to all human beings. Different groups observe that importance in different ways. From that perspective children can learn about the symbolic meaning of lights in winter celebrations and traditions: Christmas tree lights, the Menorah, farolitos, lighting candles, etc.

The holiday approach can be a very concrete way to literally celebrate differences, and if we as educators are clear about the value and limitation of the approach and go beyond that the rest of the year, then I think it has its place in the curriculum.

A word of caution: Celebrating holidays can get you into some controversial territory. Many holidays are linked to religious observances. It is difficult to separate tradition from religion, yet I do think there is a fine distinction. It is important to remember that you are teaching *about* the holiday and the people who celebrate that holiday. You are not promoting adoption of the religious values that are part of observing the holidays and rituals.

Also remember that for many children celebrating holidays and observing rituals are very important constants in their lives. Holidays give children a sense of stability, rhythm and predictability. They put some magic back into a world that sometimes has gone too much to the other extreme. Rather than eliminate these as opportunities for learning and sharing, discuss the holiday approach with the families of the children in your classroom and find out how they feel about it.

The Classroom

When I think of the ideal primary school classroom I think of a cheerful room, full of light and color. As I walk in the first things I see are the walls and bulletin boards, the posters and art on the walls.

After I notice the colorful visuals on the walls, bulletin boards and blackboards, my eyes go to the books on the shelf, the equipment, toys, puppets, props and materials that play such an important role in learning about the world.

Here is a positive and challenging environment, a place where a child is intellectually and socially stimulated, where a child feels receptive to learning, where she or he feels nurtured, safe and at home.

The following list of questions can help you assess the environment in your classroom and make it an accepting, reflective place to be.

1. What images are on the walls, posters, bulletin boards and chalkboards?

2. Do these images reflect the diversity of the children in my classroom, our school and our community?

3. Is the diversity of the United States reflected by the images that are presented?

4. Are children from diverse ethnic backgrounds represented?

5. When I use pictures of people at work, have I avoided male/female stereotypes? Are there women firefighters, construction workers or pilots? Are people of color shown as doctors, teachers and other professionals? Are homemakers both male and female?

6. Do my images represent the continuum of classes, making sure not all of them are middle class with middle class possessions?

7. Are a variety of styles of homes represented? Are there apartment buildings, mobile homes and hogans, as well as middle class tract homes and upper class homes?

8. What lifestyles am I promoting by putting these images on the walls?

9. Are differently abled people pictured doing productive, competent things, or are they engaged in passive or helpless roles?

10. Have I integrated different age groups? Are old people shown helping young people as well as young people helping old?

Once you have evaluated your classroom's physical properties, you are ready to turn to the tools you use in your work. The teaching tools and materials, toys, games and books that are used both in the early childhood and primary grade classrooms help children form their ideas about the world.

Teaching Tools and Strategies

The following tools and strategies can help you integrate information about diverse cultures into every part of your core curriculum.

Photographs and Pictures

It is still often difficult to find bias-free images of people in educational materials, although this is changing. So depending on where you get the visuals you use to supplement your teaching, be conscious about the images you are presenting.

Using magazines for collages and other class projects is an inexpensive way to incorporate visuals into classroom activities. However, a special caution is in order here. Most U.S. magazines feature images motivated by advertisers. These can be offensive to all children, but especially to children of color and differently abled children because there are few models who look like them in these publications. It is rare to see a differently abled person pictured in mainstream magazines.

I recently took part in a language arts teaching activity for a group of second graders. We received a box of magazines for our activity. The children were instructed to create a collage of nouns, cutting and pasting pictures of people, places and things. The box contained magazines such as *Vogue, Glamour, Travel and Leisure* and *Vanity Fair*.

When one boy cut out a picture of a bikini-clad blonde woman jumping off a yacht, we realized we should have screened the visuals and offered a different variety of magazines.

The houses were luxurious. Other "places" and "things" on their innocent collages were almost always things an advertiser was trying to sell. No one used pictures of people of color.

Although the children learned about nouns that day, we lost an opportunity to integrate other valuable lessons that would have contributed to their understanding of differences. With another set of magazines, the images could have been more reflective of the real world. We can't ignore the power of our props.

There are also other more subtle issues to consider when selecting visuals for the classroom.

Pay close attention to the way people of color are represented in any drawings or illustrations you use. Is there a wide variety of different facial and physical characteristics reflected within ethnic populations, or are pictures of people of color merely shaded black or brown? Are stereotypical features overemphasized in an offensive way? There is less room for stereotyping when you use photographs than there is when you use illustrations (Ramsey 1987).

On any visual aid project, make sure to include a wide variety of people of color; show different ages, weights, etc. One or two people of color does not represent diversity.

Be careful, too, about using images that are too exotic for children to relate to. *National Geographic Magazine,* for example, includes many different cultures, but children may still not be able to find images of themselves represented.

Use the following guidelines when planning visuals for your lessons:

❦ Look for magazines that reflect diversity. Some magazines that include people of color in articles and advertising include *Ebony, Hispanic, Mothering, Child, Family Circle* and *Parenting*. Sports magazines present a good range of people of color, but watch for stereotypic presentations of women.

❦ Start a clip file of photographs that reflect diversity. Ask your students and families to bring photographs of all kinds of people doing different things—people of color, women and men engaged in nonsexist activities, older people from different ethnic groups, etc.

❦ Collect photos of families from your classroom. Or have a photo day when you take your camera to school and photograph your students.

Books and Stories

Books and stories also need to be evaluated using a "diversity yardstick." The Council on Interracial Books for Children in New York City publishes a book called *Guidelines for Selecting Bias-Free Textbooks and Storybooks.* In addition to checking illustrations for stereotypes, tokenism and role depictions, the guidelines offer suggestions for what to look for when assessing children's books for racism and sexism. These include analyzing storylines, lifestyles, the relationships between people, who the heroes are and how they treat others, the images (e.g., white as beauty and cleanliness versus black as evil, menacing or dirty), the background and perspectives of the author and illustrator, and language.

A discussion about bias in U.S. history books is included as a section in the guidelines. The Council also publishes a separate book, *Stereotypes, Distortions and Omissions in U.S. History Textbooks.* (See Suggested Readings.) As ethnic groups begin to embrace their own histories, different versions of classic textbook accounts are gradually beginning to emerge. This rewriting of history is evolving and controversial. Finding out "the real story" can be challenging, but should at least be attempted as a part of any effort to create a bias-free environment for children.

Dolls and Puppets

Dolls and puppets provide a way for children to act out roles and get into others' shoes. They fit well into a range of activities, and commercial dolls are beginning to reflect more diversity. Just the other day I was browsing through a toy store and found a brown haired, brown eyed doll with light brown skin. I immediately bought it. It doesn't take much to market to me....

Still, you may not easily find multiethnic faces and differently abled dolls and puppets. It may actually save time if you make your own dolls and puppets that reflect the diversity you need for your classroom.

Making stick puppets is less involved than making dolls out of cloth. Use different shades of brown and skin tone colors, draw different facial features, use different colors for hair, etc. Glue the puppet to lightweight cardboard such as a cereal box. Then cut it out again. Paste or tape a stick to the back of it and you have a sturdy stick puppet.

After spending a few weeks in New Mexico one summer, my six year old and I came home and created a mythical small northern New

Mexico town with 12 townspeople. Each character had his or her story. There was a young Taos Pueblo girl, a Spanish friar, a Mestizo boy and many others.

We had fun acting out some of the history of the area and discussing some of the most difficult issues, such as why the Pueblo Revolt isn't called the Pueblo Defense since the Indians were defending their homeland.

Again, special caution needs to be taken when drawing pictures of people to avoid stereotypic features and details. Another way to incorporate a useful lesson is to actually find pictures with stereotypic characteristics and point them out to the children. Explain that not all people who belong to a particular group look alike.

Games

Games provide a high-interest vehicle to teach about diversity. Games have been around for thousands of years and a great majority of the world's cultures have games and toys. (The oldest board game is 4500 years old!) Games are easy to incorporate into the everyday activities of the classroom. Starting a game by talking about where it came from is an exciting new way to give children another layer of awareness and sensitivity about other cultures.

An excellent book on the universality of games is *Games of the World* by Frederic Grunfeld (Holt, 1975). Use the book to find games from other countries your students might enjoy. Or ask children to share any games they play at home or with friends. Another good activity is to assign children to interview the oldest member in their family to find out what games she or he liked best as a child.

Literature

One of the most exciting areas for teaching about diversity and promoting the acceptance of differences in the early childhood and elementary classroom is through literature. We are in a renaissance of children's literature and it is truly an exciting time for teaching and learning about diversity through literature.

Educators are recognizing that teaching reading and language skills through the use of literature is an effective way to help children master the language and develop thinking skills at the same time. More and more schools are using the whole language learning approach to teaching reading, moving away from the exclusive use of basal readers and workbooks. Adios, Dick and Jane!

Whole language learning offers countless ways of incorporating children's literature into teaching children not only to read and write but to think, to discuss, to analyze, synthesize and evaluate. With the appropriate book, these approaches can also add genuine depth to learning about diversity.

Age-appropriate literature that focuses on themes that increase children's understanding of bias-free values and introduces diversity in positive ways can spur discussion and offer practice in critical thinking skills.

For example, a teaching unit about gender might use a book like *William's Doll* by Charlotte Zolotow. In this story William wants a doll to nurture and care for. His brothers and peers tease him and his father doesn't really understand William's desire for a doll. William's grandmother understands why William needs a doll and she buys him one.

Following a whole language approach, you might first choose to read the book aloud, then ask the children to read the book to themselves. Finally, you might create different teaching activities around the various issues the book deals with.

Discussions might center around such issues as who should play with dolls and who shouldn't and why, why William's brothers and friends tease him, and how William might feel about being teased.

This is also a good opportunity to help children practice the critical thinking skills discussed in Chapter 4 by asking who, what, how and why. This story about diversity can easily be incorporated into your regular language arts program.

To help educators plan their literature programs, the California Department of Education's Language Arts and Foreign Languages Unit publishes a book entitled *Recommended Readings in Literature: Kindergarten through Grade Eight* (California Department of Education, 1988). Over 1,000 books for children are listed in this useful publication with annotations and approximate grade levels. Entries also indicate if the books are about a specific ethnic group and include contributions by African American, Chinese, Filipino, Hispanic, American Indian, Japanese, Korean and Vietnamese authors.

Story Telling

Story telling is universal. Many cultures use storytelling to pass on important values and lessons to children.

Asking children and families to participate in a storytelling project is an excellent way of enhancing ethnic/cultural pride. One way to do this is to ask children to bring in their favorite family story or folk tale. Younger children will need more help from both teacher and family so this is a very good way to reach out to families. Second and third graders will generally possess the skill to retell a story.

Older family members could be invited to class to tell the story. If some of your children don't have English language skills, you could team children up with bilingual children or otherwise obtain the aid needed to have the child actualize the activity.

A tool to help children retain the story is to have them draw some of the key people and objects in the story, color them and cut them out. Then they can make an envelope out of construction paper to keep the story pieces in. As they tell the story, they can take the pieces out to use as visual aids.

You can also use puppets and dolls to act out the story and build empathy and understanding. Often it is much easier to deal with sensitive issues through dramatic play. You can also use current events from the newspapers to tell real life stories, using these props to illustrate and keep children engaged, a much better approach than lecturing.

Tap into community resources to bring in storytellers. Senior centers and literacy volunteer projects are an excellent resource, especially if you are looking for ways to integrate different age groups into your classroom.

Chapter 4

A Safe Place: Creating a Respectful Agenda

Now that your physical environment is conducive to learning about diversity, it will be easier to address anti-bias issues more specifically. At this stage of development, however, there are still some intangibles that need to be addressed. These can be thought of as the foundation for bias-free education. This chapter focuses on three areas of educational intervention. They are creating an atmosphere of caring, enhancing self-esteem and cultural pride, and helping children think critically about diversity and anti-bias issues.

Creating this foundation will contribute to your bias-free learning environment. It will help you promote bias-free thinking and behavior. It will improve the overall climate of your classroom and school. It will help you celebrate diversity in a positive way. And it will make your classroom and school a safer place for all children to learn and grow.

Creating a Caring Atmosphere

Creating a place where children feel safe and cared for is important in any learning environment. It is essential in a bias-free classroom.

Groundrules

Agreeing on groundrules at the start of the school year is a good way to set the tone. Before you introduce the groundrules, explain to children that the main reason for the rules is to make sure we always remember to respect one another. Adapt your explanation of respect to fit the children you work with. For very young children you might simply say respect means treating everyone fairly, and not doing or saying anything that will embarrass someone else or hurt someone's feelings.

The following rules are general enough to use in any classroom. You will want to adapt them to fit the developmental level of the children you work with.

- ❧ Respect others. This means no name calling, put downs or making fun of others.

- ❧ It is not okay to leave someone out or not play with them because of what they look like or the group they belong to.

- ❧ All questions are good questions. There is no such thing as a dumb question.

- ❧ All opinions are important and worthy of being discussed.

- ❧ It is okay not to know the answers to questions. If we knew all the answers, we wouldn't have to come to school. We are here to learn from each other.

- ❧ Listen carefully and don't interrupt when others are talking.

- ❧ You don't have to answer a question or talk if you don't want to. You can say, "I want to pass."

- ❧ You can only speak for yourself. You don't know how others are feeling, or what they think.

- ❧ If you are worried about something, tell the teacher about it.

After you introduce the rules, ask children if they can think of other rules that should be added and why. Add additional rules from children, then get a commitment from the class to follow the groundrules. Explain that following the groundrules is for the good of the whole group.

Some of the concepts in the groundrules will be new to young children. You may want to create some simple activities to help them understand what some of the more abstract rules mean and how they work.

For example, you could have the children look up "respect" in the dictionary and write two or three sentences using the word. You could do a writing activity and ask them to write a paragraph about someone in their families whom they respect.

No Put-Downs: The 3-Up Rule

In our home, we use an activity that relates to put-downs. It's called the "3-up rule." Every time you put someone down, you must tell the person three things you like about him or her. So, if a put-down should slip out, one of us says, "3-up," or holds up three fingers on one hand and a thumb on the other. Without words we are saying, "I'm feeling put down by what you said and I'd like for you to take care of it." This turns the negative into a positive right away. Teachers I know report that this idea works well in the classroom as well.

Children in this age group are learning about their power and influence over others. They are discovering that they can affect others, so it is common to find them experimenting with put-downs. Clearly asserting the value that putting people down is *not* okay will teach them a skill they can use all their lives. Similarly, all the groundrules are good general guidelines for interacting with others.

The Importance of Involving Parents

Children should think of their classroom as their home away from home. For many children of color, school is a strange and frightening place. This might be the first time they feel different from others and estranged from a system vastly different from the safety of the home. Others may be encountering children of color for the first time. They may bring biases with them from their community or home.

Encouraging parents to come to the classroom, to visit and get involved, is paramount in creating an atmosphere of caring. We all know the importance of parent involvement in the schools and its relation to student success.

When trying to enhance parent involvement in a multiethnic classroom, keep in mind that in many other parts of the world, the teacher and the schools are considered supreme authorities. It is not usual for family members to question the teacher's authority. As a sign of respect for you as a teacher, therefore, parents may never question what you are doing. Even if their child is having trouble in your classroom, they may not feel comfortable coming in to tell you about it.

There is also the issue of humility. Many low income family members from third world countries may not feel they have anything to offer to their children's "American" schooling. We as educators may misinterpret parent's attitudes as "laissez faire" when actually their hands off approach may be a sign of the respect and humility they have in the face of our profession.

In a model parent participation project I worked for in South Tucson, Arizona, many of the educators reported low parent participation in the schools. We identified Hispanic parent leaders in six schools in the area and trained them to teach other parents how to participate in their children's schools. Out of this effort was born the Project YES Parent to Parent Workshops that are still being held today. These workshops are run by volunteer parents who were recruited because of the unique gifts they could offer to other Spanish speaking parents in the area.

There are special challenges in improving parent involvement when parents don't speak the language and are not assimilated into the mainstream culture. These challenges are important issues in developing bias-free education. Taking positive, culturally sensitive steps to ensure a more pluralistic representation of family resources in our communities can improve the learning environment for everyone.

Turning Parents into Teachers

Turning family members into teachers either in the classroom or in their own environment is an empowering experience for students, family members and teachers. The experience doesn't have to be academic and it can be as brief as a twenty-minute visit, once a month.

When I was in the second grade, our teacher Mrs. Kelly took us across the street to Mary Wong's house to watch her grandmother make giant flour tortillas. She had a huge round wood-burning grill set up in the back yard when we got there. I remember she didn't say a word to us as she prepared the masa. She was very old and couldn't speak English. She was probably too shy to speak Spanish. Mrs. Kelly did all the talking and told us each step in the tortilla-making process. Each of us walked back to school munching on a tortilla.

Most of us were Mexican children and we knew what tortillas were. So it wasn't that it was a new idea. The special quality of the experience was that Mary Wong's grandmother took the time to share something of herself with us—her skill.

One idea is to send home a classroom sharing list and ask parents to fill in how they would be willing to contribute to the class. Make sure to provide parent information in the language spoken in the home. If your students have family members who don't read or write, host parent nights with facilitators who speak the native language. Ask for their contributions and participation. Explain the importance of their involvement—it may be obvious to us but not to them.

Whatever your situation, it is vitally important to get parents involved, to make them feel welcome in your classroom and feel that they have something special to contribute to their child's school life and educational process.

Perhaps you have a parent who would agree to tell a story in the oral tradition or prepare a special food. Others might bring in a special fabric, toys or other objects to share with the class. Even asking a parent to come in to observe or help out once a month is helpful. Children feel proud when family members come to the classroom.

Giving Children Non-Academic Strokes

We all want our children to be capable and successful human beings. The back to basics trend in education attests to the need to give children tangible skills that can prepare them for the world of work. When our children graduate from high school we want them to be able to do more than read and write. Yet most of us are familiar with the dismal scenario of ill-prepared high school graduates who can't read at a 6th grade level. They are functionally illiterate and we're worried. In our society, in this "information age," academic competence is important.

But it is equally important to give children non-academic strokes. Giving non-academic strokes is an integral part of creating an atmosphere of caring and fostering self-worth.

School districts in some parts of the country are starting to implement "caring" curricula. One model program developed and implemented through the Scotts Valley Union School District in California is ACARE (All Children Are Exceptional). The goal of this successful program is to teach children to be more caring and nurturing to each other. ACARE provides educators with a well-thought-out program to enhance the social and emotional skills of all the children. There are several components to the ACARE program. The component that specifically addresses giving non-academic strokes is the "Bear Hug Assembly."

The Bear Hug Assembly is held once every two weeks. A caring theme is chosen and different classrooms take turns presenting the assembly to the rest of the student body. The children present skits, poems, songs, etc. During the assembly two students from each class receive Bear Hug Awards for demonstrating caring about others.

By the end of the school year each student in the school has received a Bear Hug Award. My daughter Sara came home beaming one day with her award for helping Josh with his math. She promptly exhibited her award on the refrigerator.

Receiving non-academic strokes is a self-esteem builder for all children. But for the child who isn't the best reader, the girl who can't afford Reeboks, the overweight boy who calls himself "Fatso" and the new child from El Salvador, they are precious and loving gifts. They say, "You are a worthy human being. You are valued by your teachers and peers. You belong."

Having and Expressing Feelings

Is your classroom a safe place to have and express feelings? There are two parts to this question. Is it safe to have feelings? Is it safe to express feelings? There is an important differentiation here. As North American educators, many of us embrace the philosophy that it is good to express feelings, as long as we do it "appropriately." One popular method is to encourage children to verbally express themselves using "I messages."

We need to keep in mind that not all ethnic groups support this type of direct communication. In other curriculum materials I have developed that use direct communication techniques, I introduce the "I message" technique as an optional communication tool that we use in this country. It is not the only way to express oneself. It may not be the best way.

Children from diverse ethnic groups may use many other ways to express their feelings. This is an area where it is particularly important to know your students and their backgrounds. You can help each child decide which style fits. This way the child doesn't feel pressured into adopting mainstream North American behaviors.

Have a discussion with the children you work with about expressing feelings. Communicate respect and acceptance for the different ways of expressing feelings. You can encourage acceptance for all children by explaining that we all have feelings and that feelings are not good or bad.

After you get to know the different cultures represented by your students, you will be better able to decide how to sensitively deal with accepting and expressing feelings. You are the best judge.

Once you decide that it is appropriate for the children in your classroom to learn about expressing feelings, there are some other considerations to keep in mind.

If you are trying to encourage verbal expression, remember there may be children in your classroom who may not have the vocabulary to go with their feelings. You might make lists of words that describe feelings and use them in a language arts activity.

Help children who don't feel comfortable sharing verbally by developing other outlets to help them accept, understand and express their feelings. The following are some suggestions:

- ❦ Encourage children to start a feelings journal. Make it a private activity: they don't have to share their journal with anyone— not even you.

- ❦ Have children draw different facial expressions on paper plates that indicate how they are feeling. Have them connect the plates together with yarn to make the plates into a necklace.

- ❦ Have children turn a small box into a feeling box. Have them draw different faces on each side of the box that represent angry, sad, frustrated, happy, joyful or excited feelings.

- ❦ Make an anonymous feeling box for the classroom. Have children write how they feel on slips of paper and put the papers in the box. Again, the feelings in the box aren't shared— this is a way for children to get acquainted with their own feelings with no judgment from others.

- ❦ Make yourself available after class for children who want to share a feeling with you. Tell children they can write a letter to you expressing how they feel if writing is easier than talking for them.

Self-Esteem and Cultural Differences

Increasing children's self-esteem is integral to enhancing learning in any environment. In attempting to eliminate bias, it is essential to pay attention to the self-esteem of individual children and of the classroom as a whole. Self-acceptance and acceptance of others is cyclical: the more children's esteem and confidence in themselves increases, the easier it is for them to become accepting of others.

This section provides a short discussion on self-esteem and its importance in creating a foundation for bias-free education. The discussion and recommendations here address the cultural relevance of self-esteem within a theory developed by Harris Clemes and Reynold Bean (1992). I believe this theory offers a tangible framework that is applicable across cultures.

Clemes and Bean's theory is that positive self-esteem is the result of positive feelings within four conditions. These are connectiveness, uniqueness, power and models. These four conditions are affected by the number and degree of feelings children have inside themselves (internal factors), and the factors in the environment that influence how children feel (external factors).

Very simply put, the greater the number of positive experiences—internal and external—within the four conditions, the greater the likelihood the child will have positive self-esteem. Of course the reverse is also true: negative experiences within the four conditions can decrease children's self-esteem. A brief discussion of the four conditions follows.

Connectiveness. Children with a high sense of connectiveness feel that they belong to or are a part of something that other people think highly of. Connectiveness includes:

❦ Identifying with a group of people.

❦ Feeling connected to a past or heritage.

❦ Feeling that you belong to something or someone, and that something or someone belongs to you.

❦ Feeling good about the things you feel a part of.

❦ Knowing that others respect the people or things you are related to.

❦ Feeling important to others.

Some examples of connections children might have would be to family, friends, neighborhood, church, school, ethnic group or geographic area.

Uniqueness. Children with a high sense of uniqueness feel they have characteristics that make them special and different from others. The children themselves like their own special qualities, and they know that other people (parents, friends, teachers, other adults) like them, too. Uniqueness includes:

❦ Feeling that you know or can do things no one else knows or can do (there is something special and different about you).

❦ Knowing that others think these differences are special, too.

❦ Enjoying the feeling of being special and different.

❦ Being able to express yourself in your own way.

❦ Feeling imaginative and creative because of these differences.

Some of the things children might feel unique and special about are skills or talents, background, experience and knowledge, hobbies, appearance, imagination, roles or functions.

Power. Children with a high sense of power feel that they have the resources, opportunities and abilities to control the events in their lives. Power includes:

❦ Believing you can do what you set out to do.

❦ Being able to use the skills you have to make decisions and solve your problems.

❦ Feeling excited when faced with something new, instead of apprehensive and afraid.

❦ Knowing that others can't make you do things you really don't want to do.

Children can develop a sense of power if they have the opportunity to use what they know and do well. Some resources that can help children have a sense of power are knowledge, interpersonal skills (ability to problem solve, resolve conflict, make decisions, communicate), physical abilities, a variety of experiences, and material resources.

Models. Children with a high sense of models are able to look to people they admire, respect and identify with to help them establish meaningful values, beliefs, ideals and personal standards that will help them make sense of their lives. Models includes:

❦ Knowing people you respect and want to be like.

❦ Being able to distinguish right from wrong and good from bad.

❦ Having values, beliefs and standards to guide and direct you.

❦ Knowing how to go about learning what you need to know to accomplish the tasks you need to complete.

This overview of self-esteem is meant to help make self-esteem a more tangible construct as classroom activities are planned. The following discussion and recommendations describe how each condition can be applied specifically to helping create an environment where difference is viewed as positive.

Connectiveness

Identification with an ethnic group and a sense of connection to an extended family can be a strong source of self-esteem for children when those groups are respected by others. However, once the child leaves the family (to play with other children, for example, or to attend school), feelings of connectiveness with people outside the family and ethnic group may be weakened if the child experiences discrimination based on the very groups with whom he or she feels connected.

The following activities can help children develop a sense of connectiveness:

❦ Ask children to show or share things about their families and their ethnic backgrounds as a get-acquainted activity. Watch for similar interests and common values as students are sharing, and point them out as you go along.

- Require children to work together to complete cooperative tasks. These could include projects such as large murals, plays, sports or other games.

- Group the class into small learning teams where children can get to know one another and help each other learn.

- Allow children to plan class parties, field trips or other special events for the whole class. Incorporate diversity into these projects. Play games, music or have food from different ethnic groups, for example. Visit local museums, art exhibits, concerts, etc.

Uniqueness

This condition offers a perfect opportunity to help children identify differences as positive. Unfortunately children from diverse cultural and ethnic backgrounds may have experienced negative feelings about being different if their cultural values and traditions have not been regarded as positive. You will be the best judge at measuring the uniqueness level of the children you work with.

The following activities can help children develop a sense of uniqueness:

- Encourage children to do ungraded assignments that allow personal expression: art projects, fantasy books, scrapbooks about themselves and/or their families.

- Provide opportunities to share positive ways in which children are different from one another. Some examples might be self-portraits, thumb print pictures, languages they speak, favorite things to do, different kinds of pets.

- Help children see their affiliation with an ethnic group as a source of values, pride, and as positive influence on who they are.

- Create special roles in the classroom that provide all children with some task they can accomplish in their own special way. Some examples might be monitors, helpers, announcers, organizers, role takers, timekeepers.

Note that appearance was one of the things children might feel special about. In our society, people do get validation and strokes for their physical appearance. It's important for adults who work with children to feel comfortable making observations about the physical appearances of children of color, such as the beauty of brown skin, almond shaped eyes or curly hair. These physical features are part of what makes the child a unique human being. It is important to be able to point these out with pride and confidence. Done sensitively, this can help boost a child's self-esteem.

Note: Individual uniqueness is not seen as a positive attribute in all cultures—in some cultures the individual should not stand out from the family. In these cases, reinforce the sense of uniqueness that comes from being a part of a family, a community and an ethnic group.

Power

Physical and emotional safety are essential conditions for building a sense of power in children. So the caring atmosphere of your bias-free environment is ideal for helping children who may come to the classroom with negative experiences in this condition.

The following activities can help children develop a sense of power:

- ❦ Involve all children in setting rules for the classroom.

- ❦ Help children identify their skills and abilities. (Define these terms broadly. For example, include friendliness as a skill and a sense of humor as an ability.)

- ❦ Allow children with special competences to tutor others and share their learning techniques.

- ❦ Improve personal control and use of the body through movement exercises, dance, sports, etc.

- ❦ Introduce group decision-making processes such as voting, consensus or using representatives.

- ❦ Provide clear and consistent standards of academic performance and maintain high expectations for all students.

Models

Children from diverse cultural and ethnic backgrounds may be exposed to very few examples of success whom they can model themselves after. Especially in the media, success is often defined in terms of money, glamour, political power, athletic prowess, and so on. Few models in these areas are members of diverse cultural and ethnic groups. (See the introduction for a discussion of Robert Vargas' *El No* model.)

The following activities can help help children develop a sense of models:

- ❦ Emphasize visible, everyday role models. Parents, older siblings and other extended family members, as well as community leaders and famous people, can provide a wider range of models of strength and accomplishment than the media provides.

- ❦ Introduce children to leaders from diverse cultural and ethnic groups.

- ❦ Discuss guidelines for classroom behavior and standards for grading work with children. Establishing these guidelines as soon as possible provides clear and consistent models for success in the classroom.

- ❦ Provide children with age-appropriate models for making decisions, setting goals and resolving conflict.

Thinking Critically About Differences

Racism, classism, sexism and the rest of the "ism-chasm" are difficult issues that no one likes to deal with directly. But to teach children about diversity, we must help them think about these issues. To embark on this exploration, we need to help children think critically about the world around them, particularly as it applies to issues of diversity. One easy way to define critical thinking is to think of it as teaching children the who, what, how and why of the matter.

There is some educational debate on whether young children to age ten are capable of conceptualizing another person's point of view. Patricia Ramsey in her book, *Teaching and Learning in a*

Diverse World: Multicultural Education for Young Children (Teachers College Press, 1987), states that young children do have the capacity to respond to another person's emotional experience. That is why, for example, teaching children about bias-free thinking through literature is so appropriate. It is especially appropriate in kindergarten through third grade where children are constantly exposed to the magic of children's literature.

Another important point that Ramsey makes is that children's ability to empathize with others may help them not only to understand different people but also the more sophisticated concept of social causality. Children in this age group are capable of asking who, what, how, and why if we help them.

Encouraging Children to Ask Questions

Throughout this book, we have offered suggestions on how to create a bias-free environment for young children. Many of the suggestions are relevant to the task of helping children think critically about issues of diversity and accepting differences in themselves and others. In this section, we are emphasizing the need to question mainstream values and beliefs.

We can begin to help children think critically by exposing them to the reality of others and encouraging them to ask questions. In this case the questions are as important as the answers. As their teachers and guides, we can help them find the questions to the answers. The "why is this so?" in relation to racism is just as revealing as the fact that racism exists. The same applies to all of the other "isms" of our society.

For example, as painful as it might be, we need to acknowledge to children of color that how they see themselves is being influenced by some pretty powerful mainstream values and images. We can do that by encouraging all children to be critical about what they see in books, toy stores, magazines, television and in their own play. We can watch for or set up specific situations so children can ask, "Why is this so?" By helping children see that the world may be presenting to them something they don't have to accept, we are true to our role as their guides, and we empower them.

Unfortunately, there aren't many curricula for young children that deal specifically with difficult issues like prejudice, racism, classism and sexism. Although there are some excellent resources for older children, there is still a dearth of materials specifically for the young child.

In Chapter 1, I suggested some resources to use with young children. You may have to create your own learning activities to help children with some of the more difficult issues. Again I stress the importance of knowing your children and their families as well as your community. This will help you tailor activities to the specific needs of the children you work with.

Louise Derman-Sparks' *Anti-Bias Curriculum: Tools for Empowering Young Children,* is one of the best resources I have come across. (Other helpful books about bias are listed in the Suggested Readings section.) Derman-Sparks suggests the following activity to help children explore the meaning of discrimination.

Using three ethnic dolls, help children develop problem solving skills. Set up a role play where two dolls are playing together and the third doll comes up to play. The third doll can be "different." (The way in which the third doll is different will depend on your particular classroom.) She can be rejected by her peers because she is different. This is discrimination.

Help children ask the following questions:

What is going on? (The doll is being rejected because of the way she looks.) What is this called? (It is called discrimination.) What is discrimination? (Discrimination is when someone leaves someone out or won't be friends with them just because they are different.)

Who is being discriminated against? (The different doll.) How is she being discriminated against? (The two other dolls aren't letting her play because her skin is a different color.)

Why is she being discriminated against? (She is being discriminated against because she is different from the other two dolls and they aren't used to her, or they are afraid of her.)

Encourage children to think of ways to solve this problem. What could be done to help these three dolls accept each other and get along? Stress that discrimination is unfair. Stress the importance of doing something about discrimination.

Helping Children Understand the Words

To ask questions, children need to understand the words that describe the issues. Some of the words we need to use when we talk to young children about differences are abstract and complex. The following is a list of terms that might come up, along with definitions in language children are likely to understand. You will need to adapt the terms to make them clear to the children you work with.

Stereotype. When a person thinks all the people in a certain group think or act the same way, the person is stereotyping. An example might be if someone thought everyone in the second grade was alike, just because they were all in the same grade.

Another example would be to think all girls were alike, or all boys, or all teachers, or all people who are black. It is a big mistake to stereotype others.

Prejudice. Some people decide they don't like a person before they even know him or her. They decide they don't like the person because of the way the person looks, or because of the clothes the person wears, or the color of the person's skin. Making up your mind about a person or a group of people before you know them is called prejudice.

Discrimination. Discrimination means leaving out a person, or a group of people, because of the way they look, or the clothes they wear, or the way they talk, or because they seem different to you. An example of discrimination would be if a group of girls wouldn't let a boy play baseball with them just because he was a boy. Discrimination against someone is never fair.

Culture. Culture is a way of living that we share with other members of the same group. It includes how we think, what we believe in, our customs and how we act towards others. Each of us belongs to many different cultures.

Ethnic Group. A group of people who share common culture and customs is called an ethnic group. Everyone belongs to an ethnic group. Some examples of ethnic groups in the United States are African Americans, American Indians, Vietnamese, Chinese, Mexicans and Spaniards.

Racism. Racism is putting people down, not respecting them, or discriminating against them because of the cultural or ethnic group they belong to.

Sexism. Sexism is making fun of a person or putting her down because she is a girl, or making fun of a person or putting him down because he is a boy. Stereotyping girls' and boys' behavior is another form of sexism, for example, saying "only boys do that," or "only girls do that."

Classism. Classism is deciding whether or not you like other people based on how much money they have.

These are just a few of the terms you might need in discussing these issues with children. Adapt the explanations to fit your own situation, and create your own descriptions when necessary.

When describing complex ideas to young children, keep the language and the ideas simple, and use examples when you can.

The "isms" are especially hard to explain to children because racism, sexism and classism can carry the implication of institutionalized power. Institutionalized power means that, in addition to individual beliefs or actions, the idea is a characteristic of a government or its laws, a society or its customs, or other organizations public and private. We have left this out of the definition of the children's terms. But we as educators need to acknowledge it.

Prejudice and discrimination are big issues. There are many complex reasons why we are prejudiced and why we act out against those who are different from us. Yours is a difficult job. Take your commitment to promote bias-free education seriously and one step at a time. Don't be discouraged if you can't do it all, or if you make mistakes. Take heart in the knowledge that your willingness to step out of complacency and take a stand against prejudice and discrimination presents a model for children and for other adults. This willingness represents our only hope for a changed future.

Creating a Respectful Agenda _____

Positively Different

Chapter 5

Red Flag Incidents: Responding to Stereotypes, Prejudice and Discrimination

As with other "ills" of society, prevention is the ideal way to deal with the issues of prejudice and discrimination. The first chapters of this book are devoted to helping you create an environment to help prevent the hurt and damage that prejudice and discrimination can cause. Even when your learning environment is bias-free, however, and you have followed the recommendations of this book and other anti-bias education materials and programs, you will still have to deal directly with incidents of prejudice and discrimination. This final chapter will discuss some specific ways to respond to stereotypes, prejudice and discrimination when children are involved.

A Word of Gentle Caution

Although you may feel very strongly about prejudice and discrimination, remember to be gentle with the children you have under your charge. When children make what we consider to be insensitive statements, or act out and hurt each other, we need to look at these as red flags, as needs that are being expressed.

Be kind but firm. Your minimal expectations are that children demonstrate respect for one another in class and on the playground.

When you observe children being insensitive and disrespectful to one another, refer them back to the groundrules they agreed to follow. When you establish groundrules at the beginning of the class, there are no surprises. Children feel secure when they know what is expected of them, what is considered appropriate and what is not appropriate. It is important to follow through and be consistent. Remind them that the groundrules are firm expectations of behavior and that they all agreed to follow them for the good of the whole group.

Since one of the groundrules is that all questions are okay, it is appropriate to start the next section with how to respond to the innocent questions.

The Innocent Questions

You know the ones, "How come Jody brings such weird lunches to school?" "Why does Ms. Garcia have that dirty spot on her forehead?" "Why is that lady dressed up in that funny-looking dress?"

When children ask questions out of innocence and ignorance, approach the question positively and gently. Use the opportunity to express enthusiasm for differences. Your response might be something like: "The woman is wearing a sari. Women from India wear saris sometimes. Isn't the material beautiful? It looks funny to you because it is different from what you wear. Sometimes we think things that are different are funny, but that's because we don't know how other people live. Children who live in other places might think the clothes we wear are funny, too, if they don't know anything about the way we live. After we learn about how others live, these things don't seem funny any more. They might even seem interesting."

These kinds of answers promote a positive view of differences. You are teaching children that not everyone approaches life the same way, and that this is okay. Pay close attention to the kinds of questions that come up. Children's questions can give you teaching ideas. The three sample questions might suggest lessons on ethnic foods, rituals, and why people from different ethnic groups wear different clothing.

The Big Question:
"Why Are Things the Way They Are?"

This question is more difficult to answer. It seems that a myriad of responses come to you at once and you don't know where to start. To illustrate how complex these kinds of issues can become, I will use a personal experience.

About two years ago my husband, my 5-year-old daughter and I were watching a movie about a young White girl who befriended an old Black man who lived alone in the woods. The story was set in the South. The Black man was kind to the little girl at a time when there wasn't too much kindness in her life. As the story progressed, the townspeople became aware of the little girl's visits to the old man.

The old man, realizing the implications of befriending a White girl in the South, decided to leave his home in the woods.

My daughter didn't understand why the old man had to leave. My husband told her it was because he was Black. My daughter became very upset and demanded that we tell her why. She couldn't understand why being Black was enough of a reason.

We turned the television off and explained that not long ago, Black people weren't free to choose who they befriended. We tried to explain why. We tried to explain slavery. Prejudice. The atrocities we commit out of fear and ignorance. She burst into tears, frustrated because she couldn't understand. I became irritated with her five-year-old mind that didn't comprehend the meaning of bigotry.

Looking back on that day, I think how I could have handled it differently. We all make mistakes. The important message here is that as parents and teachers, we must be open to children asking the questions, especially if the questions make us feel uncomfortable or inadequate because we don't know the answers. With practice, children will get better at asking questions, and you will get better at answering them.

When children ask why, use the opportunity to state your values. You can tell them that you feel it's wrong and unfair for people to judge others by their skin color, by the way they look, their sex or their religion. You can explain that most of the time people discriminate because they are afraid, or they don't understand, or both and that it's important that we learn to accept and respect one another. You can say that you are sometimes confused, too, about the whys. You can tell them you don't know all the answers either, but that you keep asking questions and looking for answers anyway and that they should too.

Stereotypes: "Mexican People Eat Weird Food"

> Jackie has been playing with her friend Alejandro. It's lunchtime, and Alejandro's mother offers the children a plate of menudo (tripe soup). Jackie stares down at the soup. It looks and smells different from anything she's ever eaten before. She excuses herself and goes home.
>
> "I thought you were having lunch at Alejandro's," her mother says.
>
> "I want to eat here," Jackie replies. "Mexican people eat weird food."

Jackie has formed a stereotype. Stereotypes are the images of groups of people that have become frozen in our minds. "Mexican people eat weird food" seems innocent enough coming from the mouth of a child, but stereotypes are precursors to prejudice.

Children are bombarded with stereotypes by television, advertising, movies, children's books and last but not least, family and friends.

Stereotypes come out of limited knowledge, so children are especially susceptible to stereotyping. Our young ones are grasping at all stimuli to form their definition of the world. When children notice that the vast majority of the Hispanic and Black males on television are portrayed as criminals, it is easy to form a negative stereotype. If they have little contact or interaction with the people of whom they have formed stereotypes, they will continue to hold that image and believe it to be true.

Stereotypes are the gateway to prejudice and prejudice paves the way to discrimination. So although the statement, "Mexican people eat weird food" may seem harmless, it's a clear signal to stop and explore the stereotype with the child. The statement provides the opportunity to help the child become more critical, opening her mind to other possibilities.

You might ask the child, "What seems weird about the food?" The response might be, "It looks weird," or "It smells funny." You might guide the child by saying, "It is different from what we eat, isn't it? But it's not weird. There are many different kinds of food that people eat." You might say, "To a Mexican boy, cereal shaped like moons and stars might seem weird but it's not, it's just different."

Prejudice: "The Mexicans up the Street Ate My Friend's Cat"

Gina's cat has been missing for two days. Gina is very upset. The children have been searching the neighborhood, but no one can find the cat. They are sitting on

Gina's front porch when they see Mr. Mendez working in his front yard. "I know what happened to your cat," whispers David. "I'll bet those Mexicans over there ate it! They eat all sorts of weird stuff!"

Jackie is shocked. But she remembers her reaction to the soup at Alejandro's house and begins to believe what David is saying. For days after the rumor starts, Jackie doesn't feel like playing with Alejandro because Alejandro is Mexican and she believes the Mexicans in the neighborhood ate her friend's cat.

The stereotype "Mexican people eat weird food" seeped into an innocent and absorbent young mind and led to the "Mexicans-ate-the-cat" statement. This is an example of how a stereotype turns into prejudice.

Prejudice is an attitude or thought. When it expresses itself through stereotypic statements or discriminatory behaviors, it is important to take the time to respond.

You might point out that the Mendez's don't seem like people who would eat someone's pet. Point out that Alejandro has a dog. Try to unfold the child's statement by asking why she thought this could happen. Try to direct her thinking toward the individual family and the individual people in it, and away from the general term "the Mexicans."

Discrimination: "Let's Not Play with Alejandro"

Alejandro is sitting by himself outside on the bench. Over by the swings there's a group of children giggling. Alejandro senses there's something wrong but he takes his chances and approaches them anyway. "Hey you guys want to play pirates? I'll be Captain Hook"! They run away and Alejandro hears someone say, "He's gross." Alejandro walks away and sits on the bench kicking up the dirt.

Whether it's rumors of missing cats or negative comments about different clothes or foods, stereotypes and prejudices can get implanted into the minds of children and cause discriminatory behavior. When this happens, we need to intervene by helping the child who is hurt, talking to the offenders and using the incident as a teaching opportunity.

Helping the Child Who Is Hurt

When a child is hurt by prejudice or discrimination, it's important to first give support to the child who has been hurt. Suppose you have witnessed the scene on the playground. If you turn your attention to the offenders right away, Alejandro has to wait in pain.

Walk over to Alejandro and sit next to him for a few seconds. Say nothing for a while and then give him your support. Let him know without pitying him that you know he is hurt. This is a time to explore with Alejandro. What happened? How did he feel? Explore his feelings and thoughts with him kindly and sensitively, showing him that you support and understand his feelings. Ask him why he thinks this incident happened, and what he thinks he can do to take care of himself.

At this point it is appropriate to affirm to Alejandro that it hurts to be put down. It is not okay that the children said he was gross. Let him know that you understand that it hurt and that it wasn't fair. Ask him what he thinks he can do next time.

Let Alejandro explore his own way of dealing with the situation before you provide suggestions. The solution will be more empowering if it comes from his own thinking. After exploring the options and consequences you might suggest that he could defend himself by saying something like, "I feel angry when you say I'm gross and I want you to stop!" or "I don't want to play with people who call me names!"

Talking to the Offenders

After you talk to Alejandro, you can discuss the incident with the offenders. Children can be cruel without knowing how much they are hurting each other. If you can, discreetly take the offenders aside and go through the same exploration process. You could start by saying something like, "I noticed that you ran away from Alejandro and called him gross when he wanted to play with you." Ask the children if they remember the groundrule about not putting people down. Ask them if they understand what that means.

Listen to them. What is their understanding of the groundrule? Help them speak freely about how they feel. Then ask them to tell you what happened with Alejandro. Look for the parts of the situation that you perceive differently. This will help the children understand the situation and what is expected of them. Discuss with the children how this might apply to other incidents.

Ask the children how they think they can deal differently with the situation the next time something like this happens. At this point, they may need help from your direct suggestions. You might inject your expectations of their behavior and state your values: "It's not okay to put people down. Calling Alejandro gross was putting him down and that isn't okay. If Alejandro has done something to hurt you or make you angry, it's okay to tell him how you feel about what he did. If you need help sorting out these kinds of situations and feelings, you can come to me and we can solve the problem together."

Give children the message that you feel they are capable of solving their own problems, but at the same time make yourself available to help. Try to help the children explore possible solutions so that you aren't placed in the position of lecturer.

It's important to explore with children what happened, how it felt and what they can do differently even if it is easier to tell them what you want them to do. This allows the children to think of other options themselves rather than always relying on an adult to give them the answers. Children are capable of finding their own answers. We need to guide them toward exploring the options and consequences of their behavior.

Exploring What Happened: A Teaching Opportunity

If you teach, you can use a red-flag incident as an opportunity for the whole class to learn about offending others. Wait for a few days after the incident. Then remind children of the groundrule (no put-downs or making fun of others) and make up an incident that illustrates how the groundrule might be broken. Ask the children what everyone involved might do to make sure it doesn't happen again.

If you are a parent and a similar situation arises, you can use the same technique of exploration to help children develop their own skills in dealing with these difficult issues. If your child has been the target of racism and discrimination, it is important to validate his or her feelings. "That must have really hurt you deep down." It is important for you to tell the child how you feel about it. "I'm very angry that he would say such a thing to you. It's hurtful and wrong."

Share your values with your children. If you have experienced discrimination, tell them about your experiences. What did you do? What did you learn? How did you handle it? How would you have done things differently? Children can and do learn from our experiences.

If your child has been the target of racism and/or discrimination at school, it is very important to speak up! Go to the teacher and principal and express your concerns and expectations. You aren't just defending your child. You are helping to bring about positive change.

Watching for Patterns of Prejudice

Isolated and recurring incidents are both red flags to alert you to what children need. Looking for patterns can give you more insight into the unique needs of the children you work with, their family lives and your community as a whole. If you are a teacher and you notice patterns and recurring incidents of prejudice and discrimination in your class or on the playground, it is time to alert the principal and perhaps the school counselor. Tell them you are trying to do something about these issues in your own classroom and discuss with them how to involve parents and families.

Although setting up a parent community involvement program in the schools is beyond the scope of this book, it may be appropriate to start thinking about what kind of response these patterns need in relation to your school and community. What can be done on a more general scale, schoolwide, communitywide?

If you are the only teacher dealing with these issues, you could begin to feel lonely and isolated, not to mention burnt out. You will need the support of your colleagues and friends, your principal, school district and/or families. I believe that we are moving in a direction where we will be supported for these efforts. The benefits will be bountiful.

_____ *Positively Different*

References

Abbey, Nancy, Claire Brindis and Manuel Casas. 1990. *Family life education in multicultural classrooms: Practical guidelines.* Santa Cruz, CA: ETR Associates/Network Publications.

Bean, Reynold and Harris Clemes. 1977. Revised 1992. *The four conditions of self-esteem.* Santa Cruz, CA: ETR Associates/Network Publications.

Council on Interracial Books for Children. n.d. *Guidelines for selecting bias-free textbooks and story books.* New York: Council on Interracial Books for Children.

Cummings, Marlene A. 1974. *Individual differences: An experience in human relations for children.* Madison, WI: Madison Public Schools.

Deman-Sparks, Louise. 1990. *Anti-bias curriculum: Tools for empowering young children.* Washington, DC: National Association for the Education of Young Children.

Grunfeld, Frederic. 1975. *Games of the world.* New York: Holt.

Lipson, Greta Barclay and Jane A. Romatowski. 1983. *Ethnic pride.* Carthage, IL: Good Apple, Inc.

Ramsey, Patricia G. 1987. *Teaching and learning in a diverse world: Multicultural education for younger children.* New York: Teachers College Press.

Vargas, Roberto and Samuel Martinez. 1984. *Razalogia: Community learning for a new society.* Oakland, CA: Razagenta Associates.

Zolotow, Charlotte. 1972. *William's doll.* New York: Harper & Row.

Suggested Readings

Books for Adults

Abbey, Nancy, Claire Brindis and Manual Casas. 1990. *Family Life Education in Multicultural Classrooms: Practical Guidelines.* Santa Cruz, CA: ETR Associates/Network Publications.

Allport, Gordon W. *The Nature of Prejudice.* 1979. Reading, MA: Addison-Wesley Publishing Co.

California State Department of Education, Office of Intergroup Relations. 1977. *Guide for Multicultural Education Content and Context.* Sacramento, CA: California Department of Education.

California State Department of Education. 1988. *Recommended Readings in Literature: Kindergarten Through Grade Eight.* Sacramento, CA: California State Department of Education.

Council on Interracial Books for Children. n.d. *Guidelines for Selecting Bias-Free Textbooks and Storybooks.* New York: Council on Interracial Books for Children.

Council on Interracial Books for Children. n.d. *Stereotypes, Distortions and Omissions in U.S. History Textbooks.* New York: Council on Interracial Books for Children.

Cummings, Marlene A., Karen London et al. 1981. *Individual Differences: An Experience in Human Relations for Children.* Madison, WI: Madison Public Schools.

Derman-Sparks, Louise. 1990. *Anti-Bias Curriculum.* Washington, DC: National Association for the Education of Young Children.

Diagram Group. 1975. *The Way to Play.* New York: Paddington Press Ltd.

Hernandez, Hilda. 1989. *Multicultural Education.* Columbus: Merrill Publishing Co.

Kendall, Frances E. 1983. *Diversity in the Classroom.* New York: Teachers College Press.

Lipson, Greta Barclay and Jane A. Romatowski. 1983. *Ethnic Pride.* Carthage, IL: Good Apple, Inc.

Pasternak, Michael G. 1979. *Helping Kids Learn Multi-Cultural Concepts.* Champaign, IL: Research Press Co.

Phinney, Jean S. and Mary Jane Rotheram, editors. 1987. *Children's Ethnic Socialization.* Newbury Park, CA: Sage Publications.

Ramsey, Patricia G. 1987. *Teaching and Learning in a Diverse World: Multicultural Education for Young Children.* New York: Teachers College Press, Columbia University.

Williams, Diane. 1990. *Self-Esteem.* Huntington Beach, CA: Teacher Created Materials, Inc.

Books for Children

Aardema, Verna. 1983. *Bringing the Rain to Kapiti Plain*. New York: Dial Books for Young Readers, a division of E.P. Dutton. (African American folktale, grades 1-4).

Aardema, Verna. 1979. *Who's in Rabbit's House*. New York: Dial Books for Young Readers, a division of E.P. Dutton. (African-American folktale, grades 2-5).

Aardema, Verna. 1978. *Why Mosquitoes Buzz in People's Ears: A West African Tale*. New York: Dial Books for Young Readers, a division of E.P. Dutton. (African American Folktale, grades 1-4).

Aliki. 1976. *Corn Is Maize: The Gift of the Indians*. New York: Harper & Row Jr. Books Group, a division of Harper & Row, Publishers, Inc. (American Indian informational nonfiction, grades 3-6).

Aliki. 1988. *A Weed Is a Flower: The Life of George Washington Carver*. Englewood Cliffs, NJ: Prentice-Hall. (African American biography, grades 2-4).

Atkinson, Mary. 1979. *Maria Teresa*. Carrboro, NC: Lollipop Power Books, a division of Carolina Wren Press. (Hispanic fiction, grades 3-6).

Bang, Molly. 1983. *Ten, Nine, Eight*. New York: Greenwillow Books, a division of William Morrow & Co., Inc. (African American picture book, grades K-1).

Baylor, Byrd. 1986. *The Desert Is Theirs*. New York: Macmillan, Inc. (American Indian informational nonfiction, grades K-3).

Baylor, Byrd. 1986. *Hawk, I'm Your Brother*. New York: Macmillan, Inc. (American Indian historical fiction, grades K-3).

Baylor, Byrd. 1972. *When Clay Sings.* New York: Scribner. (American Indian poetry, grades K-5).

Brooks, Gwendolyn. 1956. *Bronzeville Boys and Girls.* New York: Harper & Row Jr. Books Group, a division of Harper & Row Publishers, Inc. (African American poetry, grades 2-6).

Bunting, Eve. 1986. *The Happy Funeral.* New York: Berkley Publishing, an affiliation of G.P. Putnam's Sons. (Chinese fiction, grades 5-6).

Clayton, Edward. 1989. *Martin Luther King: The Peaceful Warrior.* New York: Archway. (African American biography, grades 4-6).

Clifton, Lucille. 1978. *Everett Anderson's Nine Month Long.* New York: Henry Holt & Co. (African American picture book, grades K-2).

Clifton, Lucille. *Some of the Days of Everett Anderson.* New York: Henry Holt & Co. (African American picture book, grades K-2).

Coerr, Eleanor B. 1979. *Sadako and the Thousand Paper Cranes.* New York: Macmillan, Inc. (Japanese historical fiction, grades 4-6).

Cohen, Barbara. 1988. *Thank You, Jackie Robinson.* New York: Lothrop, Lee & Shepard Books, a division of William Morrow & Co., Inc. (African American fiction, grades 5-7).

Courlander, Harold. 1982. *The Crest and the Hide and Other African Stories.* New York: The Putnam Publishing Group. (African American folktales, grades 4-6).

DePaola, Tomie. 1980. *The Lady of Guadalupe.* New York: Holiday. (Hispanic folktale, grades 4-6).

Feelings, Muriel. 1974. *Jambo Means Hello: Swahili Alphabet Book.* New York: Dial Books for Young Readers, a division of E.P. Dutton. (African American picture book, grades 3-6).

Fox, Paula. 1973. *Slave Dancer.* New York: Bradbury Press, an affiliation of Macmillan, Inc. (African American historical fiction, grades 5-6).

Franchere, Ruth. 1988. *Cesar Chavez.* New York: Harper & Row Jr. Books Group, a division of Harper & Row, Publishers, Inc. (Hispanic biography, grades 4-8).

Gates, Doris. 1976. *Blue Willow.* New York: Penguin. (Hispanic fiction, grades 4-5).

Goble, Paul. 1984. *The Gift of the Sacred Dog.* New York: Bradbury Press, an affiliation of Macmillan, Inc. (American Indian folktale, grades K-3).

Goble, Paul, and Dorothy Goble. 1970. *Red Hawks' Account of Custer's Last Battle.* New York: Pantheon. (American Indian historical fiction, grades 5-8).

Greene, Bette. 1975. *Philip Hall Likes Me, I Reckon Maybe.* Dell Publishing Co., Inc., a division of Bantam Doubleday Dell Publishing Group, Inc. (African American fiction, grades 4-6).

Greenfield, Eloise. 1986. *Honey I Love: And Other Love Poems.* New York: Harper & Row Jr. Books Group, a division of Harper & Row Publishers, Inc. (African American poetry, grades 3-8).

Hamilton, Virginia. 1968. *House of Dies Drear.* New York: Macmillan, Inc. (African American fiction, grades 5-6).

Keats, Ezra J. 1976. *The Snowy Day*. New York: Puffin Books (Penguin). (African American picture book, grades K-1).

Kroeber, Theodora. 1973. *Ishi, Last of His Tribe*. New York: Bantam Books. (American Indian biography, grades 5-7).

Lewis, Thomas P. 1983. *Hill of Fire*. New York: Harper & Row Jr. Books Group, a division of Harper & Row Publishers, Inc. (Hispanic historical fiction, grades 2-3.)

Lipsyte, Robert. 1978. *Free to Be Muhammad Ali*. New York: Harper & Row Jr. Books Group, a division of Harper & Row, Publishers, Inc. (African American biography, grades 4-6.)

Lord, Bette B. 1986. *In the Year of the Boar and Jackie Robinson*. New York: Harper & Row Jr. Books Group, a division of Harper & Row Publishers, Inc. (Chinese fiction, grades 4-6.)

Maury, Inez. 1976. *My Mother the Mail Carrier. Mi Mama la Cartera*. Norah Alemany translator. New York: Feminist Press at the City University of New York. (Hispanic fiction, grades 2-4.)

McCunn, Ruthanne L. 1983. *Pie-Biter*. San Francisco: Design Ent. (Chinese historical fiction, grades 4-8.)

McCunn, Ruthanne L. 1989. *Thousand Pieces of Gold: A Biographical Novel*. Boston: Beacon Press. (Chinese historical fiction, grades 5-8.)

Miles, Miska. 1985. *Annie and the Old One*. Boston: Little, Brown & Co. a division of Time, Inc. (American Indian fiction, grades 2-8.)

Musgrove, Margaret W. 1976. *Ashanti to Zulu: African Traditions*. Illustrated by Leo Dillon and Dianne Dillon. New York: Dial Books for Young Readers, a division of E.P. Dutton. (African American picture book, grades 3-6.)

O'Dell, Scott. 1987. *Island of the Blue Dolphins*. New York: Dell Publishing Co., Inc., a division of Bantam Doubleday Dell Publishing Group, Inc. (American Indian historical fiction, grades 5-6.)

Politi, Leo. 1986. *Song of the Swallows*. New York: Macmillan, Inc. (Hispanic informational nonfiction, grades 1-5.)

Politi, Leo. 1973. *The Nicest Gift*. New York: Scribner. (Hispanic picture book, grades K-8.)

Rosario, Idalia. 1981. *Idalia's Project ABC—Proyecto ABC: An Urban Alphabet Book in English and Spanish*. New York: Henry Holt & Co. (Hispanic picture book, grades K-2.)

Saiki, Patsy Sumie. 1977. *Sachie, a Daughter of Hawaii*. Honolulu, HI: Kisaku. (Japanese historical fiction, grades 4-6.)

Santa Elena, Antonio E. 1985. *Mahinhin: A Tale of the Philippines*. El Cerrito, CA: Downey Place. (Filipino historical fiction, grades 4-8.)

Scott, Ann H. 1967. *Sam*. New York: McGraw-Hill, Inc. (African American picture book, grades K-3.)

Sonneborn, Ruth. 1987. *Friday Night Is Papa Night*. New York: Penguin. (Hispanic fiction, grades 2-4.)

Steptoe, John. 1986. *Stevie*. New York: Harper & Row Jr. Books Group, a division of Harper & Row, Publishers, Inc. (African American fiction, grades 2-3.)

Takashima, Shizuye. 1971. *A Child in Prison Camp*. Pittsburgh, NY: Tundra Books of Northern New York. (Japanese biography, grades 4-6.)

Taylor, Theodore. 1989. *Cay*. New York: Doubleday. (African American historical fiction, grades 5-6.)

Uchida, Yoshiko. 1985. *A Jar of Dreams; The Best Bad Things;* and *The Happiest Ending* (trilogy). New York: Macmillan, Inc. (Japanese historical fiction, grades 4-8.)

Uchida, Yoshiko. 1982. *Journey Home*. New York: Macmillan, Inc. (Japanese historical fiction, grades 4-6.)

Uchida, Yoshiko. 1985. *Journey to Topaz*. Berkeley, CA: Creative Arts Book Co. (Japanese historical fiction, grades 4-6.)

Udry, Janice M. 1970. *What Mary Jo Shared*. New York: Scholastic, Inc. (African American picture book, grades K-1.)

Wolf, Bernard. 1988. *In This Proud Land: The Story of a Mexican-American Family*. New York: Harper & Row Jr. Books Group, a division of Harper & Row Publishers, Inc. (Hispanic informational nonfiction, grades 4-8.)

Yarbrough, Camille. 1979. *Corn Rows*. New York: The Putnam Publishing Group. (African American fiction, grades 3-6.)

Yashima, Mitsu, and Taro Yashima. 1977. *Momo's Kitten*. New York: Penguin. (Japanese picture book, grades K-3.)

Yashima, Taro. 1976. *Crow Boy*. New York: Penguin. (Japanese fiction, grades 3-7.)

About the Author

Ana Consuelo Matiella, MA, is an editor and staff writer for ETR Associates in Santa Cruz, California. She is series editor for ETR Associates' Latino Family Life Education Curriculum Series and wrote two of its curricula, *Cultural Pride* and *La Familia*. Ms. Matiella is also the author of *The Multicultural Caterpillar: Children's Activities in Cultural Awareness; We Are a Family: Children's Activities in Family Living;* and editor of *Family Life Education in Multicultural Classrooms: Practical Guidelines.*